Kenneth

Hakeem Olajuwon

by Mark Stewart

ACKNOWLEDGMENTS
The editors wish to thank Hakeem Olajuwon for his cooperation in preparing this book.
Thanks also to Integrated Sports International for their assistance.

PHOTO CREDITS
All photos courtesy AP/World Wide Photos except the following:

Rob Tringali, Jr./Sports Chrome — Cover, 6, 26
Spalding® — 43

STAFF
Project Coordinator: John Sammis, Cronopio Publishing
Series Design Concept: The Sloan Group
Design and Electronic Page Makeup: Jaffe Enterprises, and
        Digital Communications Services, Inc.

LIBRARY OF CONGRESS CATALOGING-IN-PUBLICATION DATA
Stewart, Mark.
     Hakeem Olajuwon / by Mark Stewart.
       p. cm. – (Grolier all-pro biographies)
     Includes index.
     Summary: Covers the personal life and basketball career of the Nigerian-born center for the
Houston Rockets.
     ISBN 0-516-20141-7 (lib. binding)—ISBN 0-516-26003-0 (pbk.)
     1. Olajuwon, Hakeem, 1963–   —Juvenile literature. 2. Basketball players—United States—
Biography—Juvenile literature.
(1. Olajuwon, Hakeem, 1963– . 2. Basketball players. 3. Nigerian American—Biography.)
I. Title. II. Series.
GV884.O43S84 1996
796.332'092—dc20
[B]   96-5106
                                                                                                        CIP
                                                                                                        AC

The Grolier All-Pro Biographies™ are produced in cooperation with
        Sports Media, Incorporated, New York, NY.

Grolier **ALL-PRO** Biographies™

Hakeem Olajuwon

by
Mark Stewart

CHILDREN'S PRESS®
A Division of Grolier Publishing
New York • London • Hong Kong • Sydney
Danbury, Connecticut

Contents

Who

Am I?

In the country where I was born, my name means Always Being On Top. But when I came to America to play basketball, I had to start at the bottom. Where I grew up, basketball was not a popular sport. In fact, I had only been playing a couple of years when I came to the United States, and I was not very good. By watching others and working hard, I eventually became a college All-American and an NBA All-Star. My name is Hakeem Olajuwon and this is my story . . . "

"I finally lived up to my name and made it to the top."

Hakeem Olajuwon
#34

Growing Up

Hakeem Olajuwon grew up in Nigeria with his five brothers and sisters. Hakeem's parents are both over six feet tall, and one of his brothers grew to a height of 7' 5"! Like all of the Olajuwon boys, Hakeem was very tall for his age. His quickness and height made him an excellent soccer goalie. His long arms and great balance gave him a big advantage in team handball, which is a favorite sport among Nigerians. These same skills make Hakeem one of the best centers in basketball today. But when Hakeem was growing up, almost no one in his country played the game!

Hakeem's parents owned a successful cement business in the Nigerian capital of Lagos. Hakeem's mother, Abik, and his father, Salaam, expected the Olajuwon children to stay out of trouble and respect their elders. Even though his parents were often too busy to keep an eye on him, Hakeem still behaved himself. It is customary in Nigeria for people in the community to discipline the children of others if they catch them doing something wrong. So if Hakeem got into trouble, he would actually be punished twice—once by strangers, and again by his parents after they found out!

Hakeem loved sports. His parents did not. They believed that every hour spent playing games was an hour that might be better spent studying. Hakeem and his older brother, Yemi Kaka, would sometimes tiptoe out of the house and walk over to the National Stadium. There they would sneak in and play soccer on the immense field. Although Hakeem never played much basketball, he was selected to play on Nigeria's national junior basketball team at the age of 17 because he was nearly seven feet tall. When the team traveled to a tournament in South Africa, Hakeem met a man named Chris Pond. Pond was involved in a special student exchange program called "Partners of America." He thought he could arrange a scholarship for him at a top university in the United States. Hakeem's parents realized that this strange game called basketball might not be such a bad idea after all. If Pond could get their son a free education in America, then Hakeem could play basketball to his heart's content!

A crowded city bus in Hakeem's hometown of Lagos.

School Days

Hakeem Olajuwon attended an elementary school near his home. He was a good reader and enjoyed most of his classes. Math was his weakest subject, but he asked a lot of questions and received the extra help he needed to pass. When Hakeem was 12 years old, his parents decided he should go to the Muslim Teachers School. It was so far away that he would not be able to live at home. Hakeem loved his family, and he knew everyone in his neighborhood. He was afraid of going to a place where he knew nobody. But Hakeem was able to make new friends quickly, and he got used to his new surroundings.

A student at an Islamic school receives instruction from a teacher.

Some schools in Nigeria are very crowded.

Hakeem's favorite class was English literature. He loved to read about strange, fascinating people who lived in faraway places. His teacher was very easy to talk to and encouraged him to read on his own. Hakeem also enjoyed reading about African history. When he learned that the continent's great kings and kingdoms had rivaled those of Europe and Asia, it made him proud to be an African.

"I learned how to cope with any difficulties I encountered in school by asking the right questions of the right people. Teachers are there to help you understand things and improve your abilities—once I understood that, I never had any problems I couldn't handle. Next to sports, my favorite thing to do in school was to read. If I could tell children one thing, it would be 'Learn to read and then don't stop.' Not being able to read is like living in a darkened room."

By the time Hakeem was 16 years old, he had grown to 6' 9". One day, the school's soccer coach got angry at Hakeem and told him to take a break and go over to the basketball courts. He had never played much basketball and wasn't really sure why he had been sent there. After a few minutes, he wandered back to soccer practice and told

Only ten years after he learned to play basketball, Hakeem was a star in the NBA.

Although Hakeem grew up tall, he had to develop basic basketball skills in order to compete against great pros like Chicago's Scottie Pippen.

the coach he had no interest in basketball. The coach was furious that Hakeem had disobeyed him. He ordered the young man to return to the court and stay there until he developed an interest. Little did he know that his punishment of Hakeem would forever change the face of basketball!

College

In the fall of 1980, Hakeem and Chris Pond boarded a jet in Lagos. They flew across the Atlantic Ocean to visit American colleges. Their first stop was St. John's University in New York. Hakeem was impressed with the school's campus and liked the people he met, but that evening the temperature dropped into the 40s. It never got that cold back home in Nigeria! Hakeem told Chris Pond: "Let's go to Houston."

And that is how Hakeem Olajuwon came to Houston, Texas. Hakeem enrolled at the University of Houston too late to

Although Hakeem learned to play basketball as a teenager, he outplayed many college players who knew the game from an early age.

Years

Hakeem spelled his name "Akeem" while in college, but later changed to "Hakeem."

play for the Cougars basketball team as a freshman. Instead, he concentrated on his studies and tried to improve his raw basketball skills in practice. Meanwhile, Hakeem was very homesick.

"My mother was afraid I would starve to death without my favorite Nigerian meals, like *fufu*—a meat stew served over dough—and *dodo*, which is kind of like fried bananas. Of course, I did not starve. In fact, once I discovered chili, barbecue, fried chicken, and ice cream, I actually began to gain weight. I really needed to—when I first came to America I was 6' 11", but I only weighed 180 pounds!"

Hakeem's first season with the Cougars was a learning experience. He had only been playing two years, while his teammates and opponents had been playing almost all of their lives. By his second season, however, Hakeem began to put it all together. The Cougars made it all the way to the national championship game with Hakeem playing brilliantly at center. He was named the outstanding player in the 1983 NCAA Tournament, but he came away disappointed as North Carolina State University beat Houston 54-52 on a last-second basket.

The next year, Hakeem led Houston to the NCAA championship game, but Houston lost again. Hakeem wondered what more he could do to win a championship. Perhaps his luck would change once he graduated and began his NBA career.

Hakeem and Clyde Drexler were the stars of the Cougars basketball team. Hakeem admired Clyde for his strong work ethic. They would face

Hakeem led the Houston Cougars to the NCAA championship game in 1983, but they lost to North Carolina State.

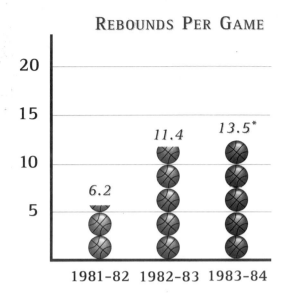

REBOUNDS PER GAME

	1981-82	1982-83	1983-84
	6.2	11.4	13.5*

*Led nation

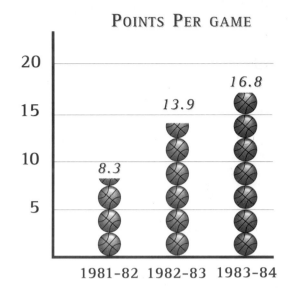

POINTS PER GAME

	1981-82	1982-83	1983-84
	8.3	13.9	16.8

each other many times in the NBA, but their finest moment in the pros came after they were reunited more than a decade after their college days at the University of Houston.

"I had been approached by several NBA teams to turn pro before my senior year, but I promised my parents that I would stay in college and graduate. My basketball career would only last so long, and I realized that without a proper education my future would be limited. It is so important to study and learn as much as you can when you are young. You never know when you will need those skills."

The Story

Hakeem Olajuwon was the first player selected in the 1984 NBA draft. The Houston Rockets thought so much of Hakeem that they chose him instead of Michael Jordan. Hakeem was happy to be able to play in the only city in America that he already knew. The Rockets had a record of 29 wins and 53 losses the year before Hakeem joined them. During his first year with the team, they improved to 48 wins and 34 losses. Hakeem finished second to Michael Jordan in the Rookie of the Year voting, leading some to wonder whether the Rockets should have taken Jordan instead. But the very next season, the Rockets made it all the way to the NBA Finals behind Hakeem's incredible play.

Hakeem was the first player chosen in the 1984 NBA draft. Here, he poses for photographers with Houston Rockets team owner Charlie Thomas.

Continues

"Twin Towers" Hakeem and Ralph Sampson (left) battle the Boston Celtics in the 1986 NBA Finals.

Although the Rockets lost the 1986 NBA championship to the Boston Celtics, they had much to be proud of. Hakeem was the best on the team, but there were many other good players. Ralph Sampson, who was 7' 4", played beside Hakeem. Fans called these two giants the "Twin Towers," after New York's World Trade Center. Two other key players were veterans Robert Reid and Allen Leavell. They had helped Hakeem when he was just learning the game in college.

Many years passed before Hakeem got another chance to win the NBA title. The Rockets had good teams and Hakeem blossomed into one of the league's best players, but the "chemistry" of that 1986 season was missing. The Rockets were tempted to start all over again and trade Hakeem for a bunch of young players, but then something magical began to happen.

Hakeem battles Patrick Ewing in the 1994 NBA Finals. The Rockets defeated the New York Knicks for the NBA championship.

Hakeem and Clyde Drexler celebrate a win over Phoenix on their way to the 1995 NBA championship.

The team hired a new coach at the end of the 1991-92 season. The following year, the Rockets won their division. The year after that, they won 21 of their first 22 games and finished 1993-94 with a record of 58 wins and 24 losses. Hakeem was voted the league's Most Valuable Player and the Rockets won the NBA championship. In 1994-95, the team recovered from a slow start to make the playoffs again. Midway through the season, the team traded for Hakeem's old college teammate, Clyde Drexler. With Hakeem and Clyde leading the way, the Rockets pulled off several dramatic comebacks to win it all for the second year in a row! "It was a thrill to be reunited with my friend and former college teammate, Clyde Drexler."

Timeline

1980: Enrolls at the University of Houston

1976: Enrolls at Muslim Teachers School in Lagos

1984: Makes the NCAA championship game for the second straight year; drafted by the Houston Rockets

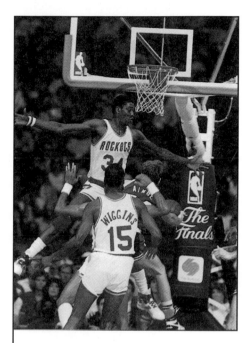

1986: Leads the Rockets to the NBA Finals

1994: Leads Rockets to first NBA title

1995: Rockets repeat as NBA champions by sweeping the Orlando Magic in the NBA Finals

1990: Wins second consecutive rebounding championship

Game

T he key play in the 1994 NBA Finals was turned in by Hakeem at the end of Game Six. John Starks of the Knicks took a last-second shot that might have won it all. When Hakeem saw the hot-shooting Starks get the ball, he jumped over and stretched as far as he could to tip the shot and prevent it from going in. The play is considered by many to be the greatest blocked shot in basketball history.

"I try to do whatever it takes to win, whether that means scoring, rebounding, or blocking shots. I do whatever I can to help."

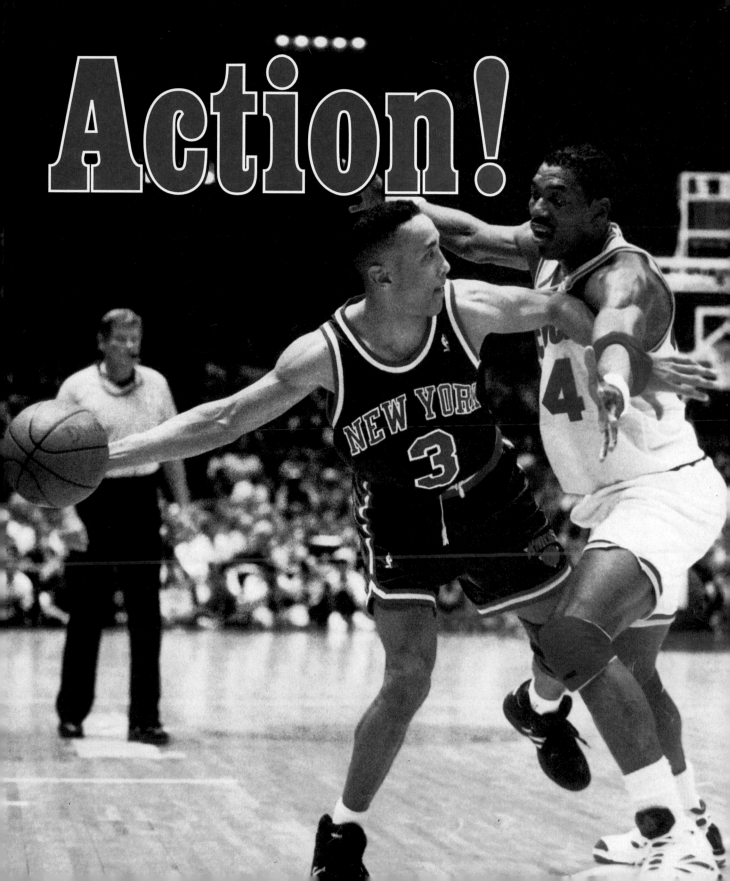

Action!

Hakeem had one great game after another during the 1995 playoffs, averaging 10.3 rebounds and 33 points a night over 22 games. He dominated regular-season MVP David Robinson to boost the Rockets into the NBA Finals. There, he outplayed Shaquille O'Neal in Houston's stunning four-game sweep.

Although David Robinson (left) is one of the best centers in the NBA, he was no match for Hakeem during the 1995 playoffs.

Hakeem "arrived" as an NBA center when he outplayed the legendary Kareem Abdul-Jabbar in the 1986 playoffs. The Rockets' easy 4 games to 1 series win put them into the NBA Finals.

Hakeem blocks a shot by Kareem Abdul-Jabbar.

Dealing

During a 1990 game against the Chicago Bulls, Hakeem Olajuwon and Bill Cartwright were battling for a rebound when Cartwright's elbow struck Hakeem in the eye. Everyone on the court could hear a loud crack, including Hakeem. He could tell from the pain that he was badly hurt for the first time in his life. X rays revealed that he had broken the orbital bone around his eye.

Chicago's Bill Cartwright leaps over an injured Olajuwon. Hakeem broke a bone near his eye and was carried off the court.

With It

During the two months his injury took to heal, Hakeem did not know how to occupy himself. "I had to wear a big eye patch. It is very scary when you lose your sight, but it also makes you more thankful for the rest of your senses. My time away from the game made me a more intelligent player and it made the team better. My teammates learned that they had the talent to be competitive without me. I began to see that if I shared more of the scoring responsibilities, we could be a team and not just a bunch of individuals."

Hakeem leaves the hospital after eye surgery.

HOW DOES

Hakeem is one of the best ball handlers in the NBA, but in college he had trouble dribbling the ball.

The weakest part of Hakeem Olajuwon's game has always been his ball-handling. This is not unusual for centers, who are rarely asked to dribble the ball. What is unusual about Hakeem is that he has been working on his dribbling skills several hours a week for the last 15 years. He used to be so bad that he often dribbled balls off his feet. Today he rates right up there with the NBA's top ball-handling big men, such as David Robinson, Vlade Divac, and Vin Baker.

"I chose to work hard on ball-handling so there would be no restrictions on my game."

He Do It?

Hakeem's ability to shoot accurately from many different angles gives him a big advantage. It means he can get a high-percentage shot off with just a little bit of jumping room. Hakeem creates his own space by faking quickly back and forth to his left and right. As he executes this move, he watches his man to see how he reacts. If the defender backs off, Hakeem will go right up with a twisting jumper. If the defender goes for one of the fakes, Hakeem will blow past him for an easy dunk.

After putting a move on Patrick Ewing, Hakeem goes up for a jump shot.

The Grind

Hakeem Olajuwon gets through the NBA's exhausting schedule by thinking of it as a test. He focuses on playing his best every night in order to show his fans that when you give every ounce of effort you have toward achieving a goal, you can accomplish some extraordinary things. This is not always easy. Nagging injuries and constant travel make it difficult to be "up" for every game. And because he follows the Islamic religion, there is a period from mid-February to mid-March called Ramadan during which Hakeem cannot eat during the day. That means he must play more than a dozen games a year on an empty stomach!

Hakeem is one of more than two million followers of Islam in the United States. Worldwide, there are close to a billion Muslims. The period of fasting called Ramadan is one of the "five pillars"—or duties—of the religion. The others include helping the poor and traveling to the Saudi Arabia city of Mecca during one's lifetime.

**President Bill Clinton receives a ball from Hakeem during
a White House ceremony celebrating Houston's NBA championship.**

"The hardest thing about being a professional athlete is having to compete and give 100 percent every night of the season. People have extremely high expectations. But the way I see it, I am in a position to inspire others. What a beautiful position to be in! How can I not want to give my best?"

Family

Hakeem leaves the court after
a busy night of hoops.

In the locker room, Hakeem is
usually the center of attention.

Hakeem Olajuwon's parents are retired and still live in Nigeria. His brother, Yemi Kaka, and sister, Kudi, also live there. Since Hakeem came to Houston, however, his other brothers— Akin, Tajudeen, and Afis—have moved to the city, too. They all live nearby. Hakeem also has a young daughter named Abisola.

Matters

Hakeem was a guest at a computer company's booth at a show in New York. Hakeem is interested in computers.

When Hakeem first joined the Rockets, his parents purchased a VCR and asked him to send videotapes of his games to their home in Lagos. Hakeem did as he was asked, but sometimes he would be so upset after bad games that he would forget to send the tapes. As a result, his parents only got to see his best games. Until they figured out what was going on, they thought their son was scoring 35 points and pulling down 20 rebounds every single night!

Say What?

What do basketball people say about Hakeem Olajuwon?

"What more can you say about him? He's just a magnificent person and player. He's a true warrior out there."

—Rudy Tomjanovich,
Houston Rockets coach

"He's a special kind of player. He hustles every second he's out there."

—Clyde Drexler, Teammate

"He's an extraordinary man. He's a sensitive, concerned human being . . . a true leader."

—*David Stern, NBA Commissioner*

"He's the best player in the world."

—*Robert Horry, Teammate*

Not only is he the best big man in the game . . . he's the best player."

—*George Karl,*
   Seattle Supersonics coach

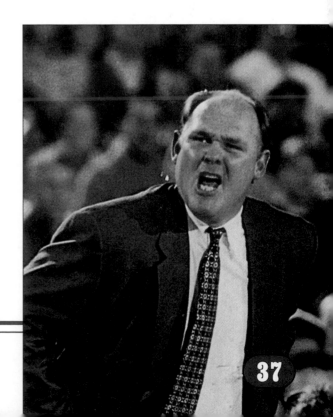

Career

Hakeem's greatest game came during the 1987 playoffs. He scored 49 points and hauled down 11 offensive rebounds in a heartbreaking double-overtime loss to Seattle.

In 1994, Hakeem became the only player in history to be the NBA's regular season MVP, Defensive Player of the Year, and Finals MVP in the same season.

Highlights

Hakeem became an American citizen on April 2, 1993. That made him eligible to play for the U.S. basketball team in the 1996 Olympics. Not surprisingly, he was one of the first players chosen by "Dream Team" coach Lenny Wilkens.

Hakeem was selected as MVP of the NBA Finals in 1994 and 1995. He is the only center in history to receive this honor two seasons in a row.

Hakeem led the league in both rebounds and blocks during the 1989-90 season.

Hakeem is the Houston Rockets' all-time leader in points, rebounds, blocks, and steals. Hakeem has been voted the NBA's top defensive center five times. He has been named NBA Defensive Player of the Year twice.

Reaching

If a special cause touches Hakeem Olajuwon, you can count on him to respond like a real pro. When civil war nearly destroyed the African country of Rwanda, he helped raise money for sick and starving refugees by taping a series of television and radio commercials.

Helping children achieve their goals is also important to Hakeem—so important, that he started The Dream Foundation. Whenever the Rockets arrive in a new city, Hakeem drops by a local junior high school and talks with the kids about staying focused on their schoolwork and aiming high in life. The organization also provides scholarships for high-school graduates in Houston.

Volunteers carry food donated by the United States to victims of the Rwanda civil war.

Out

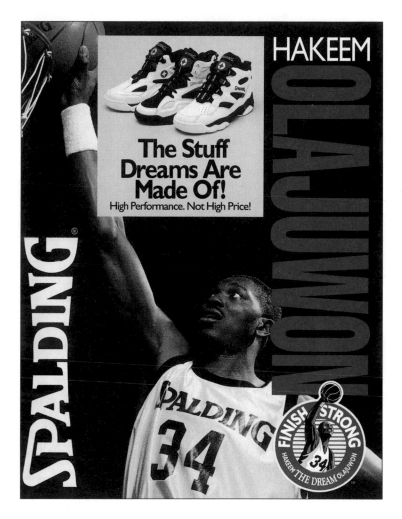

HAKEEM OLAJUWON

SPALDING

The Stuff Dreams Are Made Of!
High Performance. Not High Price!

The ad for Hakeem's shoes. The three shoes shown sell for $45 or less.

Hakeem knows that many of his fans cannot afford to buy expensive things. When he signed a deal to have his own signature sneaker created, he turned down huge offers from several companies because they planned to sell the shoes for more than $150 a pair. He finally settled on Spalding, because the company agreed that any shoe bearing Hakeem's name would not cost more than $60.

Numbers

Name: Hakeem Olajuwon

Nickname: "The Dream"

Born: January 21, 1963

Height: 7' 0" **Weight:** 255 lbs.

Uniform Number: 34

College: University of Houston

 n November 1995, Hakeem became only the ninth player in history to record more than 20,000 points and 10,000 rebounds.

Season	Team	Games	Rebounds	Rebounds per Game	Blocks	Blocks per Game	Points	Points per Game
1984-85	Houston Rockets	82	974	11.9	220	2.7	1,692	20.6
1985-86	Houston Rockets	68	781	11.5	231	3.4	1,597	23.5
1986-87	Houston Rockets	75	858	11.4	254	3.4	1,755	23.4
1987-88	Houston Rockets	79	959	12.1	214	2.7	1,805	22.8
1988-89	Houston Rockets	82	1,105*	13.5*	282	3.4	2,034	24.8
1989-90	Houston Rockets	68	1,149*	14.0*	376*	5.5	1,995	24.3
1990-91	Houston Rockets	56	770	13.8	221	3.9	1,187	21.2
1991-92	Houston Rockets	70	845	12.1	304	4.3	1,510	21.6
1992-93	Houston Rockets	82	1,068	13.0	342*	4.2	2,140	26.1
1993-94	Houston Rockets	80	955	11.9	297	3.7	2,184	27.3
1994-95	Houston Rockets	72	775	10.8	242	3.4	2,005	27.8
Total		**828**	**10,239**	**12.4**	**2,983**	**3.6**	**19,904**	**24.0**

* Led League

What If...

I was very fortunate to meet the right people at just the right time back when I was a teenager in Nigeria. What if I hadn't? Certainly, I would not be a professional basketball player. But because I studied so many different things in school, I feel certain that I would be involved in art, architecture, or perhaps teaching. Had my NBA career been cut short by injury, the courses I took in business technology at the University of Houston would have helped me to start my own company or become a valuable employee for someone else."

Glossary

ARRIVED became popular

BLOSSOMED grew

CAMPAIGN the planned steps
 taken while working toward a
 set goal

CHEMISTRY the mixture of spirit
 and abilities working together

CONSECUTIVE in a row; one
 after another

CUSTOMARY the way something
 is usually done; of a custom

ACCURATELY exactly; correctly

APPROACHED asked

ARCHITECTURE the study of how
 buildings are constructed

DISCIPLINE to teach good behavior, often using rewards and punishment

DOMINATING ruling or controlling

ELIGIBLE have the qualities needed; able

ENCOUNTERED met

EVENTUALLY in time

EXECUTES carries out

FEATHERY light; airy

FURIOUS extremely angry

HUMBLE not thinking you are better or greater than others; not overly proud

IMMENSE huge

IMPRESSED thought something was awesome or really wonderful

MUSLIM a follower of the Islam religion

ORBITAL BONE the round bone that surrounds and protects the eye

POTENTIAL/POTENTIALLY has the ability to become

PRESTIGIOUS highly respected

RIVALED tried to be as good as, or better than, another

SCHOLARSHIP money given to a student to help pay for schooling

TECHNOLOGY the use of methods, machines, and devices

WORK ETHIC keeping high moral values while trying to reach a goal

Index

About The Author

Mark Stewart grew up in New York City in the 1960s and 1970s— when the Mets, Jets, and Knicks all had championship teams. As a child, Mark read everything about sports he could lay his hands on. Today, he is one of the busiest sportswriters around. Since 1990, he has written close to 500 sports stories for kids, including profiles on more than 200 athletes, past and present. A graduate of Duke University, Mark served as senior editor of *Racquet*, a national tennis magazine, and was managing editor of *Super News*, a sporting goods industry newspaper. He is the author of every Grolier All-Pro Biography.